GW00566613

Godalming

in old picture postcards volume 2

by
R.E. Head

European Library – Zaltbommel/Netherlands

Acknowledgements:
My grateful thanks for permission to reproduce pictures and for background information go to Ron Hanley, Paul Rutterford of Pepperpot Postcards, Percy D. Barnes, Frank Buckingham, Fr. Tony Clarke, Mrs. Ida A. Evans, Miss V. Fairbrother, Mrs. E. Holl, Mrs. C. Hubbard, Mr. and Mrs. David Morley, Jack Morris, Rev. John Partington, Mrs. Anne Smith, Mrs. Sylvia Wheeler; Godalming Museum Trust; the Headmaster, Charterhouse; Surrey Local Studies Library; Puttenham and Wanborough History Society; the Vicar and Churchwardens, Godalming Parish Church; and Godalming Town Council.
The captions have been based on information from the following works, still in print, to which the reader is commended for further study: 'The Story of Godalming' and 'Yesterday's Town' (both by John Janaway); 'A Godalming Walk', 'Godalming 400', and 'Memories of Farncombe and Godalming' (Godalming Trust, Editor David Coombes); Godalming Parish Church Guide (Alan Bott). Out of print, but in Godalming Museum, are 'Local History of Godalming' (University of Surrey occasional paper), 'From a New Angle – Charterhouse 1880-1945' (W. Veale), 'Busbridge' (Rev. H.M. Larner), 'The Little Church In The Valley' (Geraldine Candlin), and 'The Church On The Wey' (Peter Andrews).
My thanks to them, and to the photographers of the past – George West and his son, W. Harding and Adrian Harding, M. Wynne, R. Munday, J.H. Muddle, and the rest, whose work made it all possible.

GB ISBN 90 288 4965 3 / CIP

INTRODUCTION

This book is about Godalming in the period 1880 to 1930. It is not, however, a history. A history of the town in that period would tell of the decline of the staple industries of wool and leather, brewing and paper-making, quarrying and foundry work, and of its already rather limited role as a market centre for the surrounding countryside. It would tell of the growth of the semi-suburban housing on all sides and latterly of service industries. Those changes, and the earlier rise and fall of other trades on which the town has depended, such as the coaching trade in the turnpike era, when Godalming was handily placed halfway from London to Portsmouth, have all been thoroughly expounded by real historians, notably John Janaway and David Coombes in their books which are still available in the bookshops. Moreover, I am a photographer rather than a historian. So, while it inevitably touches on these happenings of real history, to the extent that they form the basis of the life of the period, this book is a snapshot album depicting scenes relevant to the life of Godhelmians in the half-century 'the day before yesterday'.

Volume I, to which this book is a companion (though it stands quite independant) was published in 1985. Its 76 pictures, though many more than had up to then been made available to the public, outside of the library or museum, were necessarily selective and left out a good many pictures I should have liked to include. And subsequent to its publication I have been shown and allowed to copy many more old postcards and other old pictures of the period. So when European Library invited me to produce a second volume, I accepted gladly.

Volume I took the form of a walk around Godalming and Farncombe, with only one or two breaks in the geographical continuity. Volume II adopts a different plan, partly because of its gap-filling role. Among the aspects now covered, there are some pictures of schools and schoolchildren; a substantial section on churches — a natural subject for postcard publishers; some pictures related to the growing importance of motor traffic; and, by way of contrast with the life of ordinary people, a few pictures of Charterhouse, local stately homes, and pretty scenes on the periphery of the town. The reader will find many references to pubs and beer, for which I offer the apology that they were all plentiful in Godalming, being as much a part of the life of the period as television is a part of ours. But none of these subjects, except for the churches, really has a 'section' of the book — rather the story has been allowed to develop through various chance linkages or connections.

Our Victorian and Edwardian forebears used postcards much as we use the telephone. It was possible, if one caught a morning collecton, to send a card to another part of town, telling the addressee that one would call about teatime that day, and have every confidence that it would be delivered by the afternoon post. Cards were accordingly issued in considerable numbers and, thanks in part to the hobby of postcard collecting keenly followed at the time, many of them survive today. I have been able to select from several hunderd.

The choice is not, however, as wide as all that. Inevitably, some places, such as the High Street with the Pepperpot, the Parish Church, or the Town Bridge, appear time and again, on cards differing only slightly in angle or lighting. Publishers were not insensitive to the need for variety, and used some most unlikely pictures, even of places which were not particularly photogenic, nor of much interest even today to more than a few people. Sometimes they would refurbish an earlier card by the addition of people or other 'props' – e.g., motor cars. And some cards were of scenes, such as wooded lanes, which were and are pretty but not very revealing of life at the time. Others again are of buildings which have not changed greatly, and indeed there are whole parts of the town, let alone individual buildings, which (usually happily) remain much as they were in Edwardian or even Victorian days.

As I selected pictures and wrote about them, I began to see Godalming as a place where there are islands of constancy surrounded by a sea of change. Even since Volume I appeared there have been changes, some good, some lamentable. Recently the sea of change seems to be gaining the upper hand (to mix my metaphors!). At one time, when a shop changed hands it was usually to someone in the same line of business – the five successive firms in the drapers on page 21 are a prime example. But today there is far less of this – a bookshop can turn into an estate agents' or clothes shop, and be something else again in a year. As I write, I can hear the sound of heavy machinery gouging out the new relief road between the High Street and Croft Road. No doubt it will bring benefits. But the quiet of little Pound Lane is no more; the old clapboard house behind Harts Yard is no more; the charming town house at the bottom of Brighton Road, outside which the Godalming Band had their photograph taken in 1864, is no more. Half of Bridge Street is gone, with more to follow, including the old Sun Brewery. It is against this background that it is well to look back at how things used to be. Don't misunderstand me – I am under no sentimental illusions about the 'good old days'. Godalming at the turn of the century was a dirty, smelly, rather unhealthy place, full of beerhouses where the weary workers from the tanyards or quarries or wool mills could drown their tiredness with cheap ale. But working on the book I have been reminded that for all its defects, there was a sense of community among the townsfolk, and a variety of period and style in the buildings, some of which have been there for several centuries, that seem to be fading and in danger of vanishing altogether. I hope the 76 pictures will help to reveal to new Godhelmians some of that sense of community and continuity, and will lead them to feel more part of it; and I hope that older residents will enjoy looking again at scenes they remember – and some which were before even their time.

R.E. Head

1. Godalming in the early 1880's was still mostly confined to the Wey Valley. The suburban housing now covering much of Holloway Hill, Frith Hill, Ockford Ridge, South Hill and the others was only just beginning. This charming view, looking south from Deanery Road, shows the little town in early morning light, from Great George Street on the left to the Borough Road Bridge on the right. Smoke from a thousand hearths hangs low over the houses, hotels and shops as the day begins. In the foreground, Chalk Road has not yet been built, while the railway embankment, only 25 years old, has vegetation but no trees. In the background, note the relatively bare slopes of Holloway Hill, where now are Croft Road and Summerhouse Road, and more trees, despite the elm disease of a few years ago.

A GENERAL VIEW OF GODALMING.

G. West & Son, Photo.

2. This view shows the eastern end of Godalming, looking north from South Hill. It is by George West and Son, the town's premier photographers, and dates from about 1895. In the left foreground are buildings at the Wharf: in Bridge Road, the old British School is there, but not the Technical Institute, which was built in 1896. Nightingale Road is there, centre left, and Branksome, in Filmer Grove, at that time a boy's preparatory school, but Chalk Road is a track, devoid of buildings. On the extreme right, middle distance beyond Meadrow, Llanaway Farm is still open fields. In the centre are the sidings and warehouse of the old railway station. A locomotive, perhaps just leaving with a train for London, lets out a puff of smoke.

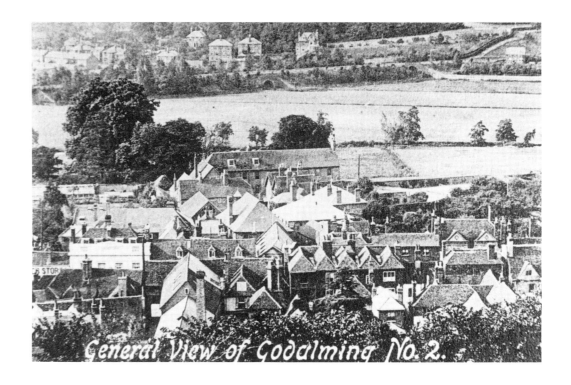

General View of Godalming No. 2.

3. This enlarged view from part of a postcard − perhaps also dated about 1895 − was taken from Holloway Hill, looking north towards Frith Hill. In the foreground are the buildings of the High Street. The Angel Hotel is the white building on the left: its classical façade appears to have been superimposed on an earlier house, a frequent practice in the past. The most noteworthy structure is, however, that covered by the long roof in the centre of the picture − this was the town's workhouse until 1843, when, already half a century old, it became redundant following a union of Poor Law districts. The vicar of the parish church, Reverend J. Bull, saw its potential and had it converted to re-house the Church of England's 'Bell' school, then in a smaller building at the Mint. The new workhouse, in Guildford, eventually became St. Luke's Hospital.

4. The old workhouse in Moss Lane served for a school for more than half a century, but by 1910 replacement was overdue. Schooling was becoming better organised and less amateur. A century of rivalry with the non-conformists had ended in 1903 when the latter's British School in Bridge Road became a Surrey County Council School, under the Education Act 1902. Moss Lane School was rebuilt, except for the master's house and the surrounding wall. The 'new schools' are the buildings there today, though the Church of England School moved in 1967 to Franklyn Road, and Moss Lane is now a County First School. There are 36 little girls in this 1910 picture — not a particularly large class for those days. The temptation to glance at the photographer has been too much for one girl. Contrast the heavy clothing, pinafores and boots with todays light sports wear!

COOKING NEW SCHOOLS GODALMING

5. 'Cooking New Schools Godalming' – we know precisely the date of this picture postcard: 3rd May 1910 is there on the blackboard, and on the original can be read with the aid of a magnifying glass. The girls are making soup, described on the board as 'very nourishing and warmth giving', making 'a good meal at small cost'. The new schools cost £5,186 to build and equip. Some of the equipment is seen here – parquet wood block flooring, electric lighting, a kitchen range to cook on, enamel bowls and pans, scales, jugs and plates, a galvanised bucket, baking tins on the mantelshelf, good solid tables and desks. Note the inkwells and pencil boxes. There were no ball-point pens in 1910!

6. Children love 'dressing up'. The sender of this postcard, on 8 june 1912, wrote to his aunty in Northampton: 'I am sending you this postcard of our Empire Celebrations at school. I am in the flag drill. Flag is half over my face. With love to all and kisses, Reg.' He is presumably the lad in the centre of the back row. So far as one can tell from the background, the school is probably Meadrow, built in 1907 as Godalming Council School. Though the flags are all British − Union Jacks for the most part − and some children are in Scottish or Welsh dress, others have clothes which may be intended to represent national dress from other parts of the Empire.

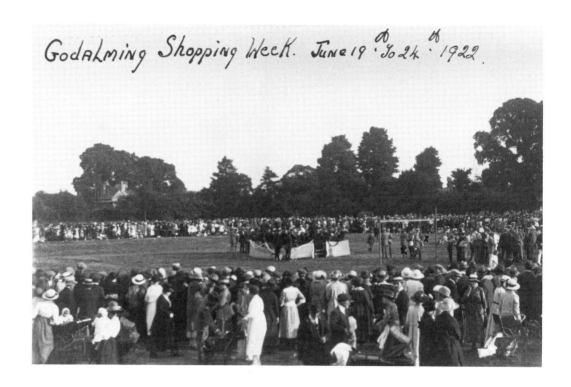

Godalming Shopping Week. June 19ᵗʰ to 24ᵗʰ 1922.

7. No doubt some of the former pupils of Moss Lane and Meadrow also enjoyed the celebration of Godalming Shopping Week in 1922. In that year the Holloway Hill recreation ground, for long the private property of the Godalming Recreation Club, was conveyed to the Borough Corporation. The novelty of its availability to anyone in the town for public events like this one may perhaps account for the large gathering at this 'sports Wednesday'. Equally, in the days before television, most entertainment was home made and anything out of the ordinary was a 'big draw'. In the centre of the arena, on the dais, a band plays: this was most likely the Godalming Band, founded in 1844.

GODALMING CARNIVAL 1924. — The Carnival Queen x Retinue.

~ ADRIAN HARDIN

8. The annual Carnival is always popular, but the 1924 Carnival was clearly something rather special among the town's celebrations. It too lasted a full week, and all proceeds went to the Royal Surrey County Hospital in Farnham Road, Guildford. A raffle for a house, built by voluntary labour out of donated materials, alone raised £950 (more than twice its market value), and there were many other fund-raising efforts. The Carnival Queen was Miss Spring, daughter of the Mayor of the Borough: he was a local timber merchant with a yard at the Wharf. The elaborate dresses of the Queen and her retinue have clearly been the subject of a lot of thought and effort, though they remind one of Cecil B. de Mille's silent film epics popular at the time.

9. The Carnival procession was a long one, in all senses of the word. It is seen here forming up in Farncombe, from where it travelled via Meadrow, Bridge Road and Bridge Street, High Street, Church Street, Chalk Road and back to the Farncombe Recreation Ground, which was also acquired for the town in 1922, by public subscription. No doubt there were some weary legs by the finish. The float on which the Carnival Queen and her attendants travelled, in relative comfort, is surmounted by a classical temple, in keeping with the style of their dresses. A small board on the wall of the house in the centre advertises the services of Mr. Gritt, the appropriately-named chimney sweep. He is remembered to have carried a bag of soot with him, to be given to any gardener who would buy him a drink.

10. The 1924 procession in the High Street, passing the windows of what is now wholly an estate agents (Hampton's), but was then still partly a clothiers. The picture was taken by Adrian Harding (whose photographer's business was located in the Barn Studio, a few doors along on the left). He set up his camera and tripod in the east window of the first floor of the Pepperpot, which commands a splendid view of most of the High Street. Flags are fluttering, clowns and footmen attend, and people crowd to watch, even on the roof of the single storey shop at the entrance to South Street. A great spectacle, fun for all.

11. Another procession, photographed from the same window, 14 years earlier, by George West or his son, whose business Harding took over about 1919. A more sober occasion, this: not a flag in sight. This procession was of 'council school' children (a term which in 1910 did not yet include those from Moss Lane, a church school), on their way to the Pepperpot to hear the proclamation of the accession of King George V, read by the Mayor from the steps. Much was to happen in the intervening 14 years. Contrast the notices on the doors of White Hart yard, on the right — in 1910 they offered good stabling, in 1924 a garage with motor-coach trips to Ascot. The single storey shop at the entrance to South Street was in this earlier picture still the garden of The Croft, the house that gave its name to Croft Road.

12. With this picture we go still further back in time. This is the High Street, from the same window seat, bedecked with flags – even the stars and stripes – ready for Queen Victoria's Diamond Jubilee celebrations. It is almost certainly a George West senior picture. The people are all making their way into the marquee that fills the street, behind the grand 'cardboard castle' front erected across the whole road between what is now Boot's Chemists and Natwest Bank. Accustomed as we are to today's heavy traffic, it seems incredible that the High Street could be totally closed in this way, even allowing for its being a national day of celebrations – consider, there was no by-pass at all, not even side streets like Croft Road, and this was the main Portsmouth Road!

13. The marquee was a very substantial affair, with wood framing, and stretched beyond the corner of Pound Lane. Here is the scene inside. The bevy of young − and not so young − ladies are decked out in their summer finery, with many ribbons and flowers. Most have straw hats − 'boaters' − as have the men on the right. The young clerical gentleman on the left could well be the curate of the parish church. The lights are interesting: the town's 1881 venture into electric street lighting, the world's first public electricity undertaking, had ended in May 1884, so the lanterns shown here may have held candles or oil lamps. If so, the fire risk must have been horrendous.

14. In Wharf Street, too, there were flags, including a couple of phoney white ensigns on a line tied to the balcony of the Conservative Club, and a picture of the Prince and Princess of Wales, later King Edward VII and Queen Alexandra. These buildings, already much altered (the porch and chimneys have been gone for some years) are threatened with demolition and redevelopment shortly. Will the new buildings include a hairdresser's? There is one there today, just as there was in 1897 – his sign is just below the right-hand white ensign. At the left edge of the picture the word 'forage' can be read on the original, on the wall of Inwoods, later Platt Bros., whose building adjoined...

15. ...the A1 Café, seen here in the 1920's. This little shop, at the corner of Bridge Street and High Street, stood about where the forecourt of the video hire shop and Halford's cycle and motor spares shop is now. The advertisements are interesting: four varieties of Will's cigarettes, with Cadbury's chocolate and Lyon's ice cream, side by side with Spratts, Spillers and Melox dog foods. The shop and café were demolished for road widening in the early 1960's. The seedsman's (and fuel) business had already transferred to T.W. Lee. At the time of writing, Lee's seedsman's and pet shop, by now in Wharf Street, was just closing down.

GODALMING.

16. Round the corner, the King's Arms Royal Hotel, here in about 1912, is a reminder of the days when Godalming was a convenient overnight coaching stop half-way between London and Portsmouth. The brick front dates from 1753, but the building it covers is in fact a good deal older. One notable visitor, in 1698, was Czar Peter the Great of Russia, with his retinue. They rather outstayed their welcome, consuming, by all accounts, a great deal more than they were willing to pay for. The coming of the railways ended the coaching trade, but partly by conversion of some of the frontage to shops, the King's Arms has survived, alone of the High Street's four principal inns of the seventeenth and eighteenth centuries.

17. One which did not survive was the Great George, the large building on the right in this picture of 1895. It was originally the George and Dragon, until the 'Little George' opened a few doors away. The name is remembered in Great George Street alongside, and the trade has continued unbroken in the off-licence on the corner. Older Godalming residents may remember perhaps that the Tea Bar, which occupies the old archway through which the coaches used to rumble, was once the 'Scotch Tea Rooms', with cakes baked on the premises. Their orange sponge is said to have been particularly mouth-watering. On the corner of Pound Lane opposite, on the left of this picture, was a butcher's business which later became...

18. ...Stovold's Eashing Farm Dairy shop, photographed here about 1930, though it remained in the firm's hands until the early 1960's, when it was run on supermarket lines. The firm, still thriving today, took pride in its modern approach and in the quality of its products. Medals were won at the Crystal Palace in 1933 and 1936 for 'pure dairy cream ices', and a milk bar − one of the first in the country − was opened nextdoor in the mid-thirties. While the Godalming shop was the main one, there was also one in St. John's Street, Farncombe. The principal business, however, was always daily milk delivery.

19. Up to the thirties, milk delivery was still mostly by horse-drawn float, as this one at Stovold's Holloway Hill depot. Petrol or diesel engines are far less suited to this work. Electric motors are better, although they are not even now as good as horses in one respect. Horses are intelligent and patient creatures, and in time some of them would get to know each house on the round, and would start and stop 'automatically', without any need for the roundsman's call to 'gee-up' or 'whoa'. The roundsman here may be Charlie Sweatman, complete with his usual cigarette, who served with the firm for many years. Note the old-style carriage lamp by his right shoulder.

HIGH STREET. GODALMING.

20. We move a little further west along the High Street from the Great George. This 1910 picture postcard, by Lloyd of Albury, was printed in Germany, like a good many others at the time. It shows clearly the granite 'setts' with which the roadway was paved. These had been acquired in 1838, at 15 shillings (75p) a ton from Guildford Borough by the town commissioners, a body set up parallel with the Borough Council. The setts were taken up in about 1913 and replaced with tarred wood blocks, but some of them were re-used almost immediately in the Phillips Memorial near the parish church. The building on the right, with ornate leaded windows, dates from Stuart times. Note the large numeral 27 on the shop on the extreme right: until it was renumbered in about 1964, the High Street was numbered consecutively, up one side and down the other. On the left, just past Thomas Rea's butchers shop, is Manchester House...

21. ...which has been successively Enticknap's, Wyeth's, Darking's, McIlroy's, and now Aspen's. The shop front has changed, but it has been same site, same building, same drapers and outfitters trade for over a century. It was Darking Bros. from 1919 to 1977, first under Mr. A.J. Darking and then, from 1931 to 1963, Mr. Geoffrey D. Brown. This postcard shows the shop in Wyeth's days before the First World War. Note the large gas lamps on their ornamented brackets: after the town's early experiment with public lighting by electricity in 1881, gas lighting was restored and continued for many years − until after the First World War in parts of the High Street and after − well after − the Second World War at the railway station.

22. When few people owned cars, shops in towns serving country districts found it paid them to deliver goods to customers. Delivery by horse and cart had, of course, been customary for centuries, and it continued for some time for milk delivery and similar start – and – stop work. But when motors became reliable enough, their greater speed led to increasing use. This model T-Ford is one of a succession of vans owned by Darkings. The young driver, here posing proudly with his van in the early 1920's, is Mr. S.E. Morley, who started working for the firm when he was 17. He came from Suffolk, but married a local girl and continued as Darking's outdoor representative for over fifty years. Note the three digit telephone number!

23. Charles Burgess was a very successful grocer whose business lasted throughout the whole period with which this book is concerned. In 1874 he took over the existing grocers on the corner of High Street and Moss Lane (formerly Moth's Lane), and it bore his name from then until it was demolished in the 1960's; a use of the site in the same trade for over a century. Opposite is Jones' the ironmongers, formerly Norris', earlier Colebrook's – another centenarian business. It too succumbed to redevelopment in the 1960's. The loss of Jones' is especially sad – the building was half of a once fine 16th century house. The remaining half, currently Natwest Bank, shows the high quality of the timber-framed building.

24. Let us glance back along the street – though later in time by a couple of decades. As mentioned, the street was then part of the main Portsmouth Road – there was no A3 by-pass. Traffic appears light in this picture, but motor cars were beginning to affect life increasingly. As early as 1904 the Borough Council had imposed a 10 mph speed limit, and in 1911 a motorist wrote to the Autocar: 'I think the unfair manner in which the speed limit is enforced in Godalming must have a very bad effect on the trade of the town. I used to spend £130 a year in the town but since the 10 mph speed limit has been worked in the way it has, I have ceased to enter the town at all.' Later, parking was forbidden on alternate sides of the street – the south side on odd-numbered dates, and the north side on even dates. The 'Angel', the third of the High Street coaching inns, here boasts a garage, with entrance by the lamppost. The Angel has now gone completely, but its name is preserved in Angel Court.

25. Godalming's Old Town Hall was built in 1814, to replace a wooden building. This had originally been erected in mediaeval times, and as well as being the seat of the town's local government had sometimes been used as a lock-up for offenders; in 1761 in the war with France, 98 prisoners had also been held there. So it is hardly surprising that by 1814 its condition should have been described as ruinous! The money for a new building was raised by public subscription, and it was built to a design by John Perry, a local architect. The Borough Council held its meetings in the council chamber on the 1st floor until 1908, when new municipal offices were built in Bridge Street. The Town Museum used the room for a number of years until its present home was provided recently. The upper storey rests upon four open arches, giving a cover for a market place at one time, and also a public convenience, until 1975, when the whole building was thoroughly renovated.

26. Tucked away behind the Pepperpot was H.T. Craddock's printing and stationery business, in the shop currently occupied by a hairdressers. Craddock was convinced that the building's presence was harmful to his business, and more than once campaigned for its removal, so that his shop, which was 'LOST, might be more easily FOUND'! It was argued that the Pepperpot was neither beautiful nor useful. Gertrude Jekyll commented: 'Perhaps it is not exactly beautiful, but its slender-pillared little clock tower and copper sheathed cupola are distinctly good, and I believe it to be the latest building in Godalming that has that precious quality of character.' The defenders won, and we still have the Pepperpot. Craddock's business cannot have suffered badly, because it too is still with us, though now in Great George Street. In 1900 it had more varied trade, including picture framing. Note the picture post-cards in the window – perhaps some of those in this book. Next door was the Grimsby Fish Stores, which later became...

27. ...Bennett's fish, game, and poultry stores. This view, from Burrow's Guide to Godalming, published in 1906, shows the shop 'decorated' with the stock, a display which the notice tells us 'won 1st. Prize in the Godalming Xmas show competition'. It was a regular event for shops to compete in this way, under the auspices of the Godalming Chamber of Commerce, and a number of similar pictures exists. The practice of hanging meat and poultry, unchilled and with no protection from flies, does not much appeal to modern susceptibilities. But at least it was the wintertime, and the pavement had been covered with paper!

Opposite Market House, Godalming.   *M. Wynne, Photo, Godalming.*

SPECIAL SHOW DAYS,

Friday & Saturday, Dec. 20th & 21st.

28. On the opposite side of the High Street to Craddock's, the White Hart was an inn from Tudor times: a date on the wall is 1571. As one of the town's coaching inns on the Portsmouth Road, both Drake and Nelson are said to have stayed there. Certainly there is documentary evidence that in 1734, General Oglethorpe, founder of the State of Georgia in the USA, brought ten Yamacraw Indians here to dine, including a chief Tomo-chi-chi. They caused quite a stir! In the yard behind the inn was a mineral water works from about 1880 to 1904. The inn itself was converted to shops in the 1930's, although the shop shown here dates from the 18th century. 'A. Jury', a hairdresser and tobacconist, also diversified his trading: in the 1920's he published picture postcards!

29. This picture is an enlargement from part of a postcard showing 'Godalming Peace Decorations'. Although the First World War effectively ended on 11th November 1918, when Germany agreed to the terms of the Armistice, it was not until the following year that the war was officially over. The sign over the furniture store (later Feltham's) proclaims a Summer Sale. There are many uniformed soldiers – perhaps preparing for a parade, or perhaps merely waiting for transport back to camp. The card was published by A.P. Taylor, of The Crescent, Milford, and there was a large Canadian Army camp at Witley Common until some time after the war – until, so the story goes, the troops grew restive at the authorities' slowness in sending them home, and set it on fire.

Godalming, High Street.

30. The west end of the High Street about 1910. The Post Office, prominent in the centre, was an 18th century town house. For many years last century Edward Stedman lived there with his family: he claimed his wine and spirits business, which he ran from the small corner shop which is now the Post Office entrance, had been established in 1811. The Red Lion public house, whose sign can just be seen, was the home in the 16th century of John Perrior, the town's first 'Warden', or mayor, after Queen Elisabeth I granted its charter on 25 January 1575. At that time, this part of the street was called Sand Street, no doubt with good reason. The motor car in the picture was not there when the photographer tripped his shutter − it was put in by the postcard's publisher to add interest! Compare its shadow, all fuzzy, with that of the bicycle alongside.

31. There is nothing fuzzy or phoney about this 1922 motor van – the first owned by the Fowle family, bakers and grocers, whose shop used to stand on the corner of Holloway Hill and Ockford Road until the early 1960's. Before the days of supermarkets and family cars most food was sold in small shops like this one. Their range was surprisingly wide, as the advertisements on the wall and window show: lemonade, ginger beer, soda-water, milk, tea, Bovril, cocoa and chocolate, and Rowntrees sweets. In the window can be identified bread, buns and cakes, apples and cucumbers. There were perhaps a dozen such shops in the town, as well as Burgesses' rather larger 'Borough Stores'. Popular motoring has changed our way of shopping as well as our way of travel.

32. The little River Ock, which rises in Busbridge and joins the Wey by the Vicarage, is only a few miles long and a few feet wide. Yet it gave its name to a mill, a Ridge and a Road — the latter seen here in an early 1900's postcard. The timbered cottages remain to this day, but the old Anchor public house, here with people standing in the doorway, was replaced in 1911 and the new building set well back from the road. The old pub had a reputation as a 'respectable and well conducted house attented by the labouring class'. The delivery boy looks natural enough, but the man with the wheelbarrow was probably engaged to stand there to add interest to the empty road. There was then, as there is now, only a high bank or wall where he appears to be heading.

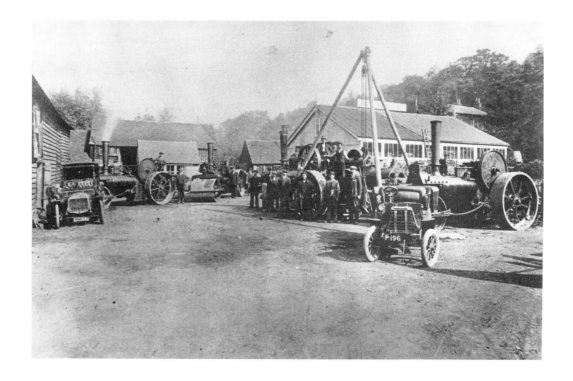

33. In 1899 Mr. F.G. Barnes bought a site opposite Ockford Mill (the new Masonic Hall has recently been built on the land), and started his garage business. The site was formerly owned by a Mr. Tomsett, a wheelwright and coachbuilder, so it was more a case of evolution than radical change of use. This picture was taken in 1906, shortly before the firm moved to their present site, the other side of the railway bridge. As can be seen, a large part of the business was then with steam traction engines and steamrollers. Growing use of the roads was beginning to call for better surfacing, in which steamrollers have a very important role.

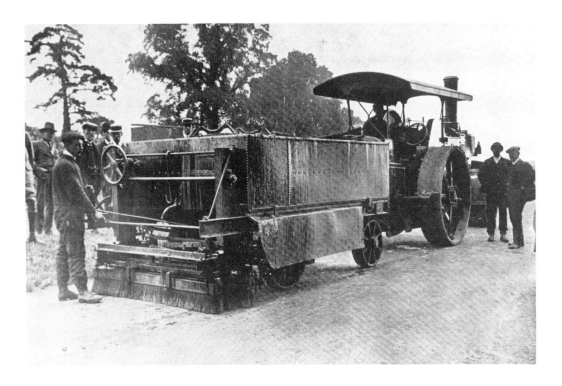

34. One way to improve the road surface and to bind the choking dust thrown up by motor cars is to spray it with hot tar, 'blind' the tar with more sand, and roll it. Heating the tar container directly with flame led to a real risk of fire − tar is very inflammable − and in an effort to overcome this Mr. Barnes developed a special machine in which it was heated by steam, supplied by the steamroller which pulled it along. The machine, which looked rather like a railway locomotive's tender, was equipped with three rows of brushes for spreading the tar. This photograph was taken at a demonstration run, on 27 May 1910, on the Portsmouth Road at Rodborough Hill. Representatives from eight local authorities, and other dignitaries were present. Two miles of road, six feet wide, were treated in about an hour. The observers must have been impressed − numbers of machines were subsequently sold. Godalming had one, and expressed full satisfaction.

Farncombe Cross.

35. As motor cars began to replace horses, garages like Barnes' began to replace the earlier forges, where smiths had hand-made and fitted shoes for horses. In some places the enterprising smith made the transition, but some never did. One Farncombe forge stood at the cross, where Hare Lane, on the left in this picture, meets Lower Manor Road, on the right, St. John's Street, and Fern Road. There are many postcards of this 'picturesque' scene, some plain, some coloured, some with and some without figures: the couple crossing the road here are patent additions. The house and forge were real enough, however. The smith's name is on the notice over the door, which also says he was a locksmith and bellhanger. Mr. Stenning was succeeded by a Mr. Sex − who later moved his forge to a site in Farncombe Street, where there is now a garage.

Farncombe Street.

WH.A.2662

36. Here is Farncombe Street, at its junction with St. John's Street, about 1910. It was then a much quieter spot, despite the nearness to the railway (the level crossing gates and signal box are just visible to the right of the more distant white building). But even then the beginnings of today's shopping parade were appearing: just beyond the Royal Oak is a grocer's, advertising Reckitts Blue (for brightening whites in laundry), and next to the railway is Pearsons the baker's, advertising Hovis bread. Between them was once a branch of Gammons, a draper, whose main shop was in Godalming High Street. This branch was managed by the parents of Jack Phillips, the wireless operator of the Titanic, who went down with the ship after staying at his post to send out S.O.S. messages. He is remembered in the Phillips memorial ground, between the Parish Church and the river.

37. This postcard probably also dates from about 1910. On the left is the sign of the Three Lions public house, still serving the thirsty today, unlike four of its neighbours in Meadrow which at that time were flourishing. Next on the left is a little corner shop, the 'Meadrow Cash Stores'. It resisted longer than most against the rising threat of competition from supermarket shopping, but recently changed from selling anything and everything to selling fancy brassware, which the supermarkets do not stock. Note the press of traffic – two carts at once! This too was part of the Portsmouth Road.

Farncombe Meadow.

38. Another of the five Meadrow pubs was the Fountain, seen in this enlargement from a postcard. It still stands, but has been converted to a shop selling newspapers and confectionery. It might be thought that its demise as a pub was related to its location — right next door to the Railway Hotel (now the Wey Inn), and it was, after all, one of 22 pubs on the main road, and as many again in other parts of the town. In reality each pub had its own clientele, for whom it served as a place of evening relaxation, and the competition that has forced them to close has come from first the cinema, and, since the war, from television. Note the delivery cart (which looks too down-at-heel to deserve the title of brewer's dray), which is one of Lascelles Tickners, a Guildford brewery: but there were once several breweries in Godalming — at least three in Bridge Street alone.

39. With so many breweries there was a steady demand for hops. The area between Godalming and Farnham was famous for them at one time. Even today a few are still grown, on the southern slopes of the Hogs Back. In this picture, taken in 1898 at Shoelands Farm, Seale, near Puttenham, a basket of hops is being emptied into a large sack, called a 'pocket', draped over a portable frame. When full, the pocket will be roughly stitched and carted off to store and eventually the brewery. The bowler hat of the man in the centre, with the cigarette, proclaims him to be the gaffer or boss: and he is, in fact, Mr. William Allden, owner of Shoelands. The man with the cap is probably the tallyman: hoppickers, mostly from London on a working 'holiday', were paid by the basket.

40. Even though wages were low, beer was cheap – 2d a pint at one time, and spirits were 2d a nip – so men would quite often be 'one over the eight' – drunk. Not only men, but women and even little children. Pubs opened at 6am and closed at 11pm. Licensing hours were only introduced nationally in the First World War, largely because the munitions workers (not in Godalming), earning good money, needed to be kept sober enough to do their job. So much drunkenness led to a reaction. The Band of Hope was an association of young persons pledged to lifelong abstinence from alcoholic drinks. Here is its Godalming 'Temple'. Note the two girl's sashes – on the left is Temperance, and on the right is Religion. There was a Band of Hope associated with the new Baptist Church Sunday School in 1903.

41. Opposite the Fountain in Meadrow was a cab station run by Mr. Isaac Nash. He used also to rent out vehicles – cabs, broughams, dog carts. His name is visible in the centre of this picture, and the photograph may well have been taken to advertise his fleet. No doubt his business was once conveniently located near to the Old Station, which was behind the builders merchants yard, lately Hooper and Ashby, now Crosleys. In 1897, however, the new Farncombe Station was opened and Godalming Old ceased to be used for passenger traffic, though it continued as a goods station until the 1970's.

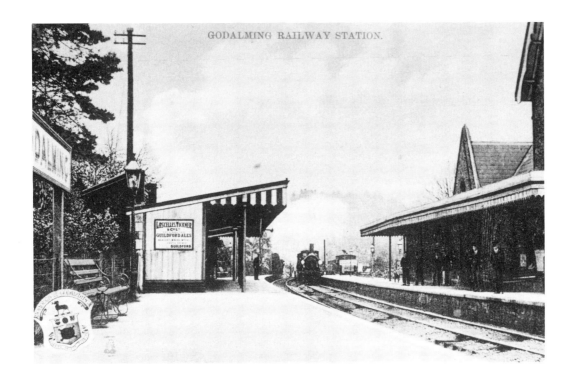

GODALMING RAILWAY STATION.

42. The railway first reached Godalming in 1849, and for ten years the old station was the terminus of the line from London. After a great deal of effort, negotiation, opposition and expense, the line was extended to Havant and Portsmouth, and opened in 1859. The new section was single track at first, the doubled track ending at Godalming New Station, where a siding (now the upper car park) facilitated rolling stock management. The main station buildings – beautifully restored recently – are still with us, but the up platform shelter, and the elegant barley sugar lampposts, went in the 1960's.

43. Before the railway age there was the canal age. The River Wey was made navigable from the Thames to Guildford under an Act of Parliament of 1671, and in 1764 a further Act led to extension to Godalming. Thus the town was a canal terminus – at the Wharf – 88 years before it became a railway terminus. The purpose was of course purely commercial. There may have been occasional pleasure boating, but it was another 130 years before boats were made available for hire for pleasure, on an organised basis. The Surrey Advertiser in June 1895 recorded that some gentlemen had combined to purchase boats for hire and that six boats had been brought from Reading. The Farncombe boating station at Catteshall Lock is with us still, letting out steel 'narrow boats' fitted out for family holidays, as well as skiffs, punts and canoes.

Eashing Bridge.

August 6th 1904.

"*Isn't this an ideal spot!*"

44. Godalming was the head of navigation, but there's more to the river than that. Eashing Bridge, a couple of miles upstream, is a venerable structure, built in the 13th century of local bargate stone, probably by the monks of Waverley Abbey. Gertrude Jekyll, in her book 'Old West Surrey', wrote of attempts to have it pulled down and replaced in the name of 'Progress', and of her delight that it had been successfully defended. We can share that delight with her and the sender of this John Valentine's postcard, posted in 1904, the year her book was published. The bridge, which is owned by the National Trust, is a favourite subject for artists, photographers and, inevitably, postcard publishers.

45. The view from Eashing bridge has changed very little over the years. These cottages were also bought by the National Trust in 1902 (for £400!), and the whole area is now protected by Green Belt restrictions on development. The public house. The Stag, then another of Lascelles Tickners, continues to thrive. The Mill, just out of sight to the right of the picture, maintains an industrial use of the site that dates back to at least the Domesday Book in the 11th century. One thing that has changed is the slope into the river, which used to give thirsty horses access to the water. It was sometimes used by carters to run their carts into the water − see previous picture − so that the wood of the wheels would swell up and keep them tight against the iron rims. But since 1904 the river has deposited a large amount of alluvial soil on this bank.

GODALMING, UNSTEAD BRIDGE

46. Unstead Bridge is a short way downriver from Farncombe boathouse. Despite its charms, the photographer has chosen to aim his camera at Unstead *farm*! He did well to do so, for Gertrude Jekyll, in her book 'Old West Surrey', describes the farm as '...one of the best and earliest examples in the country of the use of oak timber... a good sample of the work of rural builders of three hundred years ago'. The building is clearly very old. There is a record of the farm − no doubt a still earlier building on the same site − being used as a wool collecting centre in the fourteenth century.

Loseley House.

47. Roughly contemporary with Unstead Farm is Loseley House. The manor of Loseley has been in the hands of the More family, now More-Molyneux, since the days of King Henry VII. Standing about mid-way between the old boroughs of Godalming and Guildford, the house was built between 1562 and 1568 — twenty years before the Armada — mostly from the stones of Waverley Abbey, near Farnham, when that monastery was 'dissolved' by King Henry VIII. The white facings are, however, clunch, a sort of hard chalk. These stones came from a quarry in Guildford. The cost of the building is recorded — £1,640,19s,7d. The beautiful windows remind one of the saying about another Tudor mansion: 'Hardwick Hall, more glass than wall.'

48. Loseley House has outlived some other 'stately homes' in the area. Eashing House has gone, and so has this classical mansion, Busbridge Hall, shown in a photograph by a member of the first Godalming Camera Club. Built about 1650 and enlarged and improved in 1775, the Hall was demolished in 1906, when the present hall was built on a new site. The formal lake, made by damming the little River Ock, is home to many waterfowl. A magnificent avenue of chestnut trees used to line the drive to the hall, all the way from the lodge, still standing and lived in at Crownpits. The Busbridge estate belonged in mediaeval times to a family called de Bursebrugge, and their name remained associated with the estate when they sold it in 1544.

49. Another name that has stuck, albeit corrupted, since mediaeval times, is 'Crownpits'. The word is said to be a corruption of an old English word, 'crumb', meaning bent or crooked, via 'Crompett' (1548), and 'Crumpotes' (1614). The Three Crowns, seen here, was one of two pubs next to each other in Brighton Road, Crownpits, the other being the Queen's Head. Both went in the 1960's – the Queen's Head was converted into a private house, but on the site of the Three Crowns are now four town houses, all including 'Crown' in their names.

Busbridge Church.

50. Busbridge Church was commissioned as a memorial to her first husband by Emma Ramsden of Busbridge Hall. He died in 1861, just before her son Ellis Duncombe Gosling was born. The church was designed by Sir George Gilbert Scott, R.A., built by James Moon and Son, and cost £4,000. The foundation stone was laid by young Ellis when he was five years old, and the new building was consecrated by the Bishop of Winchester on 1st March 1867. The church is in Early English style, built of Bargate stone, and with the inside of the walls lined with chalk. The church is not the only memorial: local residents will recognise in 'Ramsden' and 'Duncombe' the names of two roads in the area.

51. The generosity of owners of Busbridge Hall did not end with the building of Busbridge Church. In 1910, Mrs. Percy Graham gave fine oak pews to replace the chairs seen in this picture of about that date. She also gave the oak panelling and marble pavement in the chancel and sanctuary, the marble altar rails and an alabaster reredos. Other benefactors also contributed much. The pride of the church are the embroidered silk altar frontals designed by William Morris, worked by his firm about 1870; the windows in the sanctuary and chancel and at the West End, designed by Sir Edward Burne-Jones; and the chancel screen, designed by Sir Edwin Lutyens and installed in 1899. Lutyens designed many fine houses in West Surrey and they were often complemented by gardens by Gertrude Jekyll, whose own Lutyens house at Munstead Wood is only a few hundred yards away from the church.

52. Also by Lutyens – who designed the cenotaph in Whitehall, and the Jekyll family tomb in the churchyard – is the Busbridge War Memorial, to 54 parishoners who died in the two world wars. Their names are listed on the north wall of the church. The War Memorial is 20 feet high and carved from a single block of Portland stone. The service of dedication shown here took place on Sunday 23 July 1922, at 6 pm. General Sir Charles Monro, Bart., Colonel of the Queens Royal Regiment, pulled away the Union Jack with which it had been draped, the monument was dedicated by the Rector, a wreath was placed, and the General addressed the large congregation. Three buglers from the Grenadier Guards, just visible on the left nearest the church, played the 'Last Post' and 'Reveille', and the National Anthem was sung. Gertrude Jekyll provided flowers and foliage from her garden for the service.

53. A funeral, some time around 1912, turns out of Church Street and heads for the Mint Street Salvation Army Chapel. The chapel was built in the 1830's by the Congregationalists: when they moved to their new church in Bridge Street in 1868 they sold it to the Methodists. When they in their turn moved, to Bridge Road in 1903, the chapel was at first rented by the Salvation Army and later bought by them. And so it remains. The deceased in the horse-drawn hearse was, no doubt, some prominent non-conformist Godhelmian. The band wear Salvation Army caps, but the big drum bears the words 'Godalming Band'. The sign on the wall points to Fudgers 'Empire' picture palace, in Station Road, Godalming's first regular cinema, which opened in November 1911. Up to then there had been showings of films at the Borough Hall — which is where they are back in the 1990's.

Godalming, Church Street.

54. Church Street links the Parish Church and the Pepperpot. There is saxon work in the church, and it is known that the wider area where the Pepperpot stands has been the focus of local government for a lot longer than there has been a building on the spot. It seems safe to conclude that the street, as a route, is 1,000 years old. The buildings are of course newer − the oldest perhaps half that age. In the golden years of postcards, its short length held four pubs and as many teashops. Three of the pubs are visible in this 1905 card: the house with the window box, extreme left, was the cornmeter. Also on the left, with upstairs windows open, is the Star − still with us: and on the right, just beyond the arch, is the 'Live and let live'. Apart from two houses just beyond the Star, demolished in 1912, and the garden wall visible at the far end, this view is virtually unchanged. That is, so far as buildings are concerned: the users of the shops have changed (the grocers on the left was one of the last in the town) and the houses on the right are now shops.

55. As the oldest and until recently the largest building in Godalming, quite apart from its religious significance to so many people, it is inevitable that the Parish Church of St. Peter and St. Paul should have been the subject of many postcards. The fabric of the building includes contributions from every century, from before the Norman Conquest to our own times. Though an account of its history – and it is well-documented in the church guide – is a record of constant building and rebuilding, changes are slow on such an extended timescale. This view could have been taken at any time in the last 100 years, except for the tree in front of Church House, now gone, and the early motor vehicles. The motorcycle sidecar is interesting: sidecar racers still talk of the passenger being 'in the chair'.

56. The Parish Church was restored twice last century, in 1840 and 1879. Most postcards of the interior show a view substantially the same as it looks today. This early photograph shows it as it would have been seen just before the restoration of 1879, in which the gallery and pulpit steps, and the round saxon chancel arch, were removed, and the norman chancel arch to the east of it was raised. This revealed the east window to its full height. The elaborate brass candelabra, here shown in the nave, is now in the chancel. It was made in 1722. Note the gates to the pews.

57. The vicarage includes 17th, 18th and 19th century parts. Here it is at the time of the extension on the north side at the end of the 19th century. A notice on the wooden scaffolding (held together by rope lashings) shows that the builder and contractor was John Lee of Godalming. Note that all have hats: most of the men have flat caps, although there are three or four felt hats and one, on the extreme left, which looks very like a farm labourer's hat. There are, too, a few bowlers: perhaps these were an indication of rank − charge hands or foremen. One such, perhaps Mr. Lee himself, sits next to the top-hatted gentleman in the centre of the front row, who is no less a person than the vicar, Dr. Leonard Hedley Burrows. He was vicar from 1888 to 1904, before being made Bishop of Lewes. In 1914 he became Bishop of Sheffield, which he remained until 1939.

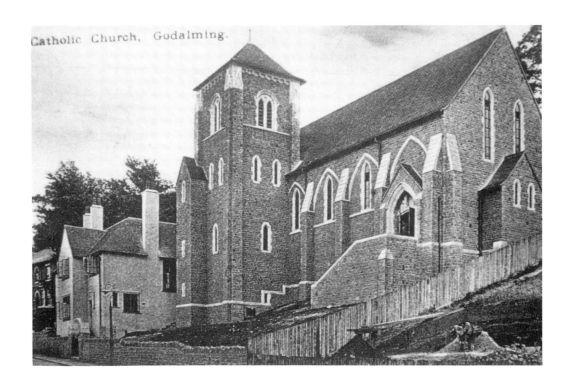

Catholic Church, Godalming.

58. In 1904, the first priest of the newly-created Godalming Catholic parish was Father Hyland. He was the inspiration and driving force behind the building in 1906 of this church, dedicated to St. Edmund, opposite his lodging at 36 Croft Road. There is a story that the hillside site was chosen so that even its short spire would be higher, and thus nearer to God, than that of the parish church in the valley. The 28 steps make attendance difficult for the infirm, however, compounded by lack of parking for cars, and in 1967 a new church was opened in Portsmouth Road, Milford. The cost of St. Edmund's in 1906 was £3,500, but it was paid off by 1923, Father Hyland being probably the main benefactor. He was later made a Canon, and remained parish priest until his death, aged 75, in 1950. He was buried under the Sanctuary of what was very much his own church.

Catholic Church, Godalming

59. A visitor to St. Edmund's in 1990 would hardly recognise it from this picture. As it shows, when first built the interior of the church was austere, but in the following year, by an anonymous gift (Father Hyland again?), the 14 Stations of the Cross were placed round the walls. These are bas-relief plaques commemorating Christ's journey to crucifiction on Calvary. There is only one other such set in the country. The present high altar was erected in 1923, the lady chapel was donated in 1930, and with very fine carved stone reredos and stained glass windows, the church has today an altogether warmer welcome for the worshipper.

60. The opening up of Queen Street in 1897 soon led to development along it. One new building was the Baptist Church. Although few in number − only 27 people were present at their foundation meeting in January 1901 − the Godalming Baptists moved quickly under their first Minister, Reverend P.A. Clements. He gave news of a site in Queen Street, with a frontage of 84 feet, costing £5 per foot. A building with a temporary end wall (to allow for later extension) was proposed and, by the end of June 1901, rough plans had been drawn. In 1902 the architect's plans were ready and builders approached. As ever, costs escalated, but in February 1903 a tender of £962 from Mitchell Bros. was accepted. No fewer than six foundation stones were laid on 6 March 1903, and on 24 June the church was opened 'A simple pleasing structure in Bargate stone, with Bath stone dressings and a cheerful red roof'. In the 1950's the church became rather overful, and a new church was planned, a dream realised in 1964. The old church is now the church hall.

61. The 1903 Baptist Church needed furnishing. A harmonium was bought for £15. A wrangle over whether to have chairs or pews was settled, eventually, and 240 chairs 'with battens' were bought at £2.6s.0d. (£2.30p) a *dozen*. Chairs without battens were then 7s. (35p) a dozen cheaper! The heating was by 'St. Patrick Gas Stoves', made in Birmingham. This picture of the interior in 1924, though less than perfect, is excusable as it is probably unique. It shows that the church was then still lit, as well as heated, by gas. The chairs, also shown here, were replaced by pews in 1927. The inscription round the arch, surrounding the blank wall for the intended later extension, is 'Unto Him Who Loved Us'.

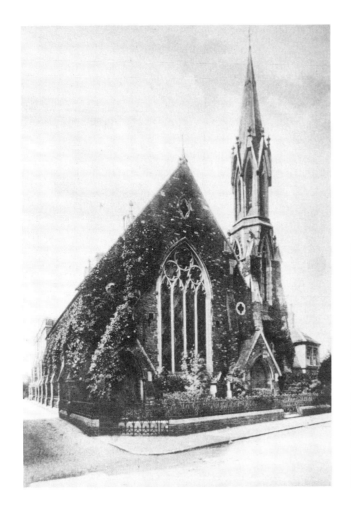

62. For nearly 150 years the Congregationalists worshipped in their church in what is now Mint Street, but in January 1867 need for more space led to a decision to build a larger church. There was no delay: under their Minister, Thomas Davies, B.A., a subscription was opened, a new site found in Bridge Street, and plans made. The subscription list was headed by Thomas Simpson Esq. with a donation of £600, but not without importance was 'thank-offering to God, £1,10s' and 'Upward and Onward £1,10s'. On 27th May 1868 the memorial stones were laid of this fine new church, designed by William F. Poulton of Reading, a popular designer of Congregational churches. And on 28th October the church was opened. It cost £3,600, including the organ. Later the house next door was bought for a manse. After a century of varying fortunes, in 1977 the Congregationalists and Methodists joined together in the Godalming United Church, and the last service in this building was held on Christmas morning. Now, its spire truncated, it is used for furniture auctions.

The Congregational School, Godalming

63. In 1879, the Congregationalists bought additional land at the rear of their new church and had this schoolhouse built. It was considered quite a showpiece, '...of which any Church might be proud. The central hall is surrounded by two tiers of classrooms, all open to the hall, and capable of being shut off by curtains for private teaching'. The architects were Welman and Street, of Guildford and Godalming. The cost, including site and furnishings, was £2,500. Coming so soon after the expense of the church, such a sum must have been a struggle to find. To judge from the picture, not a lot was spent on comfort — the seating looks rather hard!

64. Next to the Congregational Church is the Town Bridge, built in 1782, to replace the old Lord of the Manor's private bridge. Until then, the ordinary people had to use the ford alongside − even in this early 20th century postcard the slope down to the ford on the southern bank can still be made out, between the bridge and Bridge House. Bridge House was owned by a family called Marshall, whose timber yard was at the Wharf close by. The bridge was widened in 1930, following an accident in 1926 when a local builder was crushed against the parapet by a truck bringing timber from Godalming Old Station to another timber yard, Gridley and Spring, also at the Wharf.

Bridge Street, Godalming

65. Probably no part of Godalming has changed more in the last century than Bridge Street. This 1910 postcard shows what great diversity of buildings and activities it then held. On the left are clearly visible Edgington's cycle shop, West Surrey House (a pub), a dairy, Bocking's the printers and stationers, several other shops and the four-storey Sun Brewery. On the right, among others are a shop selling petrol, the newly-built council offices and Borough Hall, Fry's the builder's, and in the distance the A1 café. Many of the buildings on the left have already gone, and the rest are likely to follow soon, overwhelmed in the development of the Co-op supermarket. Some of the pictures in this book were in Bocking's 'New Shilling View Book'.

22519 Godalming. Borough Bridge.

66. At the other end of the town, the Borough Bridge is quite a substantial construction, with high arches for a shallow river which at this point carries no traffic: these earned it the local nickname of 'lunatic bridge' when it was built. In time of flood, however, much water can pass under. Through the arches can be seen the Boarden Bridge − made of boards − which for centuries was the town's only river crossing apart from Town Bridge. It still carries a public foot path.

Godalming, Borough Road and Frith Hill.

67. The Borough Bridge and Borough Road were built the early 1870's. They were an initiative of the Borough Council, stimulated by the need to improve communications at the west end of the town in connection with the coming to Godalming from London of Charterhouse School, whose new buildings on part of Deanery Farm were opened in 1872. One early trade was the twice daily supply of beer to the workers on the site, while the school was being built. The beer came from the 'Live and Let Live' pub in Church Street (see picture 54).

68. The arrival of Charterhouse was certainly much welcomed by the town's traders, and its presence has played an important part in the development of all the area surrounding it. Peperharow Road was little more than a farm track in 1872, and Charterhouse Road, seen here, centre, was then Sandy Lane. The school itself is barely visible, left skyline, and most of the large buildings prominent in the picture were the master's houses, in which the boy's were accommodated − Robinites, Bodeites and others − or ex-masters. The house just to the left of the school coat of arms is the Red House, designed for Reverend H.J. Evans by Lutyens, no less, but irreverently christened 'The Jam Factory' by the boys.

69. Here is William Haig-Brown, the great headmaster and 'second founder' of Charterhouse. He was in post from 1863 until 1897, and while he was not the first to conceive the idea of moving the school from its cramped and overcrowded London site, it was his tact, diplomacy and persistence that brought it about. It was almost certainly his idea that Godalming should be the new location. He was a man of exceptional mental powers, business-like and with a splendid memory. He handled all the correspondence and accounts of the school himself, although it grew from 200 to 500 boys in his time. He knew a great deal about each one of them, and while severe and stern when necessary, he had a considerable sense of humour and was greatly liked and respected. He was also physically strong, and absent through illness for only 12 days in his 34 years of office.

70. One of the boys who came to Godalming from London with Charterhouse was Robert Baden-Powell. He later led the successful defence of Mafeking, besieged in the Boer War. After its relief − which also relieved enormously a jingoistic British public − he was the hero of the hour. New cloisters, designed by G.D. Caroe who lived at Vann Lane, were erected at Charterhouse in memory of old Carthusians who died in the war, and Baden-Powell is here seen 'laying' the foundation stone. He published in 1908 his book 'Scouting For Boys', which led to the formation of the Boy Scouts movement, and a new role for him as World Chief Scout.

71. It is difficult for us today to appreciate the importance to Victorian England of the relief of Mafeking. Used to victories in little wars, our fathers were shaken by the unexpected strength of the Dutch Boer farmers in South Africa. 'Mafeking Night', when the news reached London of its relief, was a wild carouse for some, and there were many, if milder celebrations to follow. Here is the Godalming Recreation Club, at their Holloway Hill ground, gathered round a picture of the hero, Baden-Powell, with lots of Union Jack flags. Our picture is damaged, but is of value since every person, including some important Godhelmians, has been named on a tracing overlay. The bewhiskered figure in the centre was H. Mackey, who with his brother ran the Pound Lane forge; extreme left is J.S. Ballard, of the High Street stores; extreme right is W.H. Cooper, newsagent; and two places to Mackey's left, arm half raised, is J.N. Debenham, estate agent.

72. Distant as it is from the town, Charterhouse had to rely on its own resources for many services, especially in the early days. Here is the volunteer fire brigade surrounding their manual pump. They were in action 'for real' on 19th March 1918, when Verites house caught fire. Their efforts to contain the fire, until the Godalming and other regular fire brigades arrived to help, suceeded, in that the lower floors were saved. The brigade also gave useful service at fires in Godalming, notably the stable yard at the Kings Arms, and Murray Marshall's timber yard at the Wharf.

73. In 1904 the Godalming fire brigade — run since 1894 by the Borough Corporation, but still manned by part-time volunteers paid a shilling a week — acquired both new premises in Queen Street and this Shand Mason steam fire pump. It cost the Borough Council £285, and it is seen here, brand new and gleaming, on its acceptance trials alongside the River Wey at the Wharf. Steam powered the pump, but the engine was still pulled by horses, until about 1925, when it was altered for towing behind a motor lorry, on which the firecrew rode. The old shed seen in the background in the picture is still there, as it was in 1830, when the Wharf was in its heyday as the head of navigation.

74. The fire pump was called the 'new steamer' to distinguish it from the brigade's earlier steam pump. Its first serious use was at a fire at the Oak Bark Tannery in Mill Lane, run by Messrs. Rea Son and Fisher. Alas, the pump quickly broke down. The engineer was accused of poor maintenance and demoted, the second engineer being given his job: the whole brigade then resigned in protest! In due course peace was restored, which was as well, for as this picture shows, Rea's had another big fire only five years later. As Oscar Wilde, I think, commented about the loss of parents, one is a misfortune: two is downright careless!

75. Leather mills are a thing of the past in Godalming but in the 1900's they were a major employer of townsfolk. Rea's mill was one: Westbrook was another, seen behind the railway bridge in this picture. Leather working at Westbrook probably began in the 18th century, and was continued by the Pullmans from 1878 until 1952. This mill too had a big fire, in December 1914. But, far more important, its water wheel powered the dynamo in 1881 when Godalming became the first town in the world to have a public electricity supply. The initiative no doubt came from John Pullman, head of the firm, a town councillor and, in 1894, its mayor. Interestingly, the site of the mill has now been redeveloped as the headquarters of Messrs. Kennedy and Donkin – electrical engineers!

Godalming, Pullman's Mills from Borough Bridge.

HAND IRONING ROOM
GODALMING SANITARY LAUNDRY

76. Leatherworking was one Godalming industry; paper making, at Catteshall Mill, was another. But woolworking was the towns-folk's main occupation for centuries. One successful firm was G. Holland's 'Fleecy and Segovia Hosiery', from 1788. Less than a century later, the firm was in difficulties and in 1885 the 'Godalming Sanitary Steam Laundry' began to share their premises in Catteshall Lane. In 1890 the hosiery went and the laundry remained in sole possession, right up to the late 1970's. This turn-of-the-century card was one of several issued to advertise the business. Clearly the company was a considerable employer. This book began with Godalming's buildings: it closes with its people, who must ever be its most important resource.